Becoming a
Pioneer

Becoming a Pioneer

A Book Series

The Month-by-Month Guide
to Double your Business and
Take Over Your Industry in a Year

Bimal Shah

Book 6: Making The Biggest 90-Day Leap
Every Quarter

Becoming a Pioneer - Book 6

ISBN: 978-1-0881-5608-7 Paperback

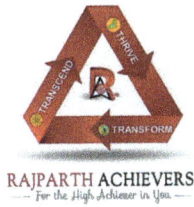

RAJPARTH ACHIEVERS
— For the High Achiever in You —

TheOneYearBreakthrough.com

For more information, email: Bimal@theoneyearbreakthrough.com

Rajparth Achievers, LLC
5550 Glades Road, Suite 500
Boca Raton, FL 33431

WHAT IS THE PIONEER CLUB FOR A BUCK?

- Buy the book for a Buck and you join the club
- Meet and network with other Pioneers
- Walk away with great results at the club meeting
- Complete the exercises in the book
- FREE Tools and Resources
- Win an invitation to the Mastermind **($495 Value)**
- Provide a great review on Amazon

https://bit.ly/ThePioneersClub

Connect with Pioneers around the World. Every Month. With the book purchase, you are a member. No strings attached.

Join Me and walk away with personalized insights for you in the monthly Club meeting.

Get Your Free Membership here.
https://bit.ly/ThePioneersClub

Learn Exponentially More.

This book is best used in conjunction with its training which allows you to
not only make The Biggest 90-Day Leap but also strategically and tactically improve your capabilities and resources to exponentially scale your business in a year.

Get Your Free Video Training at
https://bit.ly/TheBiggest90DayLeap

To my wife, Ami, and our daughters, Rajvi, and Parthvi. This book would not have been possible without the efforts of Ami with the editing. Her strength and support are priceless. Also, I am indebted to my daughters for their invaluable insight into the structure and design. My family is everything to me.

I love them with all my heart.

Content

Author's Preface

Making Pioneers! —The What and Why

What is a Pioneer?

A pioneer is unique and different from the rest.

To be a pioneer, you need to be the Only One at something. This book is about breaking all the barriers and obstacles you have in your life, work, habits, and mindset. The purpose of this book is to bring a 10x to a 100x transformation in your perspective about yourself—to assist you in realizing your true potential in a very short time.

Why be a Pioneer?

God has made every human being unique and different. When every human becomes unique and different, the whole world can work in harmony. Becoming a pioneer happens through stages and discoveries. I wrote this book with the intent to create the essential stages and discoveries you will need at each step. Drawing from my own experiences, it builds fresh perspectives that can take your business to the next level.

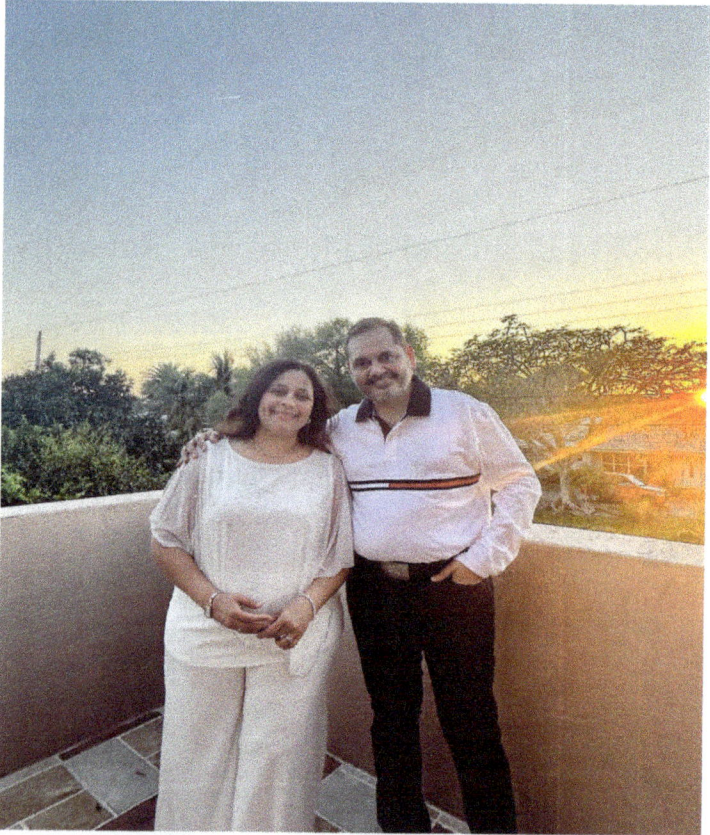

Editor Ami Shah with Author Bimal Shah

How To Get the Most Out of This Book Series

Go slow. This is a book you do not want to read fast. Write in the margins. Scribble in it, make notes and use sticky notes. Carry this book with you wherever you go. This is your book and customized manual to help you at least double what you believe you can do in a year.

Even if you answer one question from this book, it will have a positive impact on your life or business. Below are five ways you can make the most out of it:

1. Read first, think second, and then write: Read a sentence or two or a paragraph. Think about it and answer the questions that follow.

2. Go digging: Look up something in your business or your personal life related to the question. And then come back and answer the question.

3. Use Sharp Pencils with an eraser on top: Instead of using pens, please use pencils, as while you are writing your thoughts on the questions, the answers may change in due course.

4. Watch the video before you start reading: In the video, you will get a lot more insights into the book itself. It will walk you through powerful elements to scale.

5. Scan the QR CODE and save the QR CODE link in your Notes on your Smartphone: When you answer a specific question, look up the links listed in the Link Tree. See if there is a resource for the problem you are trying to solve. The Link Tree is very useful. It works like magic; you will find new and amazing things each time you look.

Special Advice for Using This Book
in Uncertain Economic Times

As we all know, the future is questionable. I recommend using this book series in a sequential order to stabilize and speed up your income growth. Follow the advice in the acronym UNCERTAIN:

U-Unique - Discover from each book how to become unique. Book #5 lists elements to leverage to be unique.

N-New – Apply the different tools and systems taught in book #1, book #9, and book #11. To bring in the new you in record time.

C-Confidence – Use the Confidence Journey tool from book #5. To build daily confidence in your journey.

E-Empathy – Use the Self-Empathy skills from book #10 and book #2 (this one). To deal with uncertainties, biggest pains, or frustrations.

R-Resilience – Lay the foundation for building resilience with a powerful vision in book #1. Apply Book #12 resiliency skills.

T-Transparency – Discover from book #3, book #4, and book #6 how to use good or bad transparency. This is to propel you and your business to the next level.

A-Audacious – From book #1, book #13, and book #6 you will discover how to maintain and chase audacious goals.

I-Implementation – From Book #7 on Sprints and Book #8 on Leadership. Throughout each book in the series, you will become a master implementor.

N-Next Steps – Every single chapter in each book helps you build your customized next steps. There is no way you can't stabilize or grow if you follow all the steps you built by yourself, using this book series.

Special Advice for Using this Book Series
in Prosperous Economic Times

When times are good, you can make them better by using this book series with the acronym AWESOME as follows:

A-Algorithms - In business when there are a lot of opportunities coming your way, you need to apply an algorithm: a one-line business plan. Build your customized scale from algorithms listed in book #4 and book #13.

W-Wins – At the end of every chapter, you celebrate your wins. In book #5 you have the tools that make it a recurring habit.

E-Extra –There is no traffic beside you in the extra mile. In book #12, you will have the systems to drive on no-traffic roads.

S-Surprisers –What to do when your team and customers surprise you. You are bound to get surprised quite often. Discover the best responses in book #1, book #2 (this book), book #3, book #4, and book #10.

O-Omnipresence –Through book #6 and book #3, you will build your systems. Through book #11 you will build your own skill sets. Through book #9 you will build the platforms. In book #10 you will have the systems and tools to automate omnipresence.

M-Multiplication –When times are good, you need systems to multiply. Through Book #1 you will lay the foundation for multiplication. Through Book #7 you will build the skills. Through Book #8 and book #9, you will build the traits for becoming a multiplier and the systems essential for it.

E-Extinguishers –When things are happening like rapid fire, you need a different kind of extinguisher. This is to extinguish the fires and keep up the pace you are moving at. Build your fire extinguishers from book #5.

Introduction

This book is written with the intent to make an immediate positive impact on you, the reader. Because of this reason, there are more questions, with immensely valuable tools, resources, stories, and action steps.

This way you can even answer one question and see a positive impact. I want you to have notes all over this book and that's why there are a lot of spaces for you to make this book your "own unique book."

There are many self-development and business books out there, but I wrote this one to direct your thinking in a specific way. So, sit back and relax while you read.

There is just one topic in this book that allows you to go deep. It also makes a real positive difference in the least amount of time. Even if you spend five minutes reading this book, you will feel the transformation.

What's unique and different about this book is that this is the book series you will cherish forever. It has your goals, your plans, your actions, and most of all a system you can use every year.

The system consists of a series of 13 stages. Each last 4 weeks; you can achieve your 3-year goal in One Year. Besides, I didn't want to write about anything you already knew.

Alongside the questions for you to answer are tools to use. And some practical solutions you can put in place and see great results.

I hope this book will make a more positive impact on your life. For your convenience, I have left you enough space for answering each question. I have noticed many people have bigger handwriting and need more space to write!

Eagerly looking forward to meeting you in Part VII!

Week 1

The Fit Business Leap

I used to wonder if there is a "fitness" evaluation for business. Now I know that in the journey of making your business fit, you could be making a meaningful transformation in your business. What I realized and learned is that you must make your business fit through 90-Day Leaps and this 90-day leap system makes your business jump to the next level in business effectively.

Let me talk about a company that used it and scaled. I was working with a restoration company that restores people's homes from water damage. We did a business fitness evaluation and discovered that the business was not fit in areas of operations, marketing, and finances. We built the 90-day leap and focused on those key areas and daily results to hit the quarterly super-green in BHAG® Goals- (Big Hairy Audacious Goals). They had a big conference room with frames. We took down the frames and converted the entire wall into a whiteboard.

We built the entire dream-come-true experience process using The Process Innovator™ tool. I have shared that tool later in this chapter. That dream-come-true experience was built after we had built the integrated vision (I talk in depth in Book # 1), we had understood how to resolve their biggest challenges (The system for overcoming challenges is shared in Book # 2), we eliminated the dangers and obstacles (Book # 3), discovered the system for capturing the opportunities (book #4), and we learned how to leverage their strengths (book #5).

When we integrated everything, we hit the green and everybody celebrated with a deep-sea fishing trip and the company went from $3M to $5M in sales in less than 6 months. That is the power of a leap. Below I will walk you through a series of questions, next steps, action items, and thinking tools to help you build "The Fit-Business 90-Day Leap."

To do this, we need to start from the basics. Which is understanding what a leap is. A leap could mean different things, but it must be unique to you and help you take it to the next level in the next 90 days. To integrate all your goals- 25-year Vision, 5-Year Moonshot, and 3-Year Goal- Book #1 will help you get clarity on defining your custom leap.

Once you have done that, you can start on the next step.

In your own words define What a leap is to you?

_____

_____

_____

_____

_____

_____

_____

According to the Merriam-Webster dictionary, a leap means to spring free form or as if from the ground. For example, a fish leaps out of the water, a young boy leaps over the fence. A leap is something that happens fast.

Once you have defined the leap, you need to write your own customized leap for a defined time frame ideally-90 Days.
What would be your biggest 90-day leap?

_____

_____

_____ _____

_____

_____

The main reason any leap would be successful is the purpose behind it. The purpose is the essential driver and can be built through the two questions below.

Why is this leap important to you?

What would be the transformation this leap will make in your life and your business?

Now that you have written your desired customized leap and the purpose, the next step is to see if you have knowingly or unknowingly leaped successfully in the past.

Do you think you are making leaps in your business? ☐ Y ☐ N

If yes, please write down the One to five areas where you are making a leap and the factors that are helping you make that leap. If No, go through Books 1 through 5 to get to the elements, structure, and thoughts that are essential in building the framework for your leap.

1. An area where I leaped or am making leaps in my business.

_____

The contributing factors:

_____
_____
_____
_____
_____

2. An area where I leaped or am making leaps in my business.

_____

The contributing factors:

_____
_____
_____
_____
_____

3. An area where I leaped or am making leaps in my business.

_____

The contributing factors:

_____
_____
_____
_____
_____
_____

4. An area where I leaped or am making leaps in my business.

_____

The contributing factors:

_____

_____

_____

_____

_____

_____

_____

5. An area where I leaped or am making leaps in my business.

_____

The contributing factors:

_____

_____

_____

_____

_____

_____

_____

Now, to make the most ideal leap, write out the one to ten areas where you want to make leaps in your business:

1._____

2._____

3._____

4._____

5._____

6._____

7._____

8._____

9._____

10._____

The reason for the above exercise is to help you make the most optimal leap you can in the next 90 days and imagine all the possibilities. "Imagination when combined with the proper knowledge and tools becomes a powerful force that can achieve the impossible." - © Bimal Shah.

Processes and systems can make everything attainable and on the next pages, I have shared The Process Innovator Tool and a sample with instructions to build processes you would need for the leap.

<u>Instructions on How to Use The Process Innovator™ Tool:</u>

The outcome of the Tool: Imagination is more powerful than knowledge. While using this tool, you are not worrying about the possible, you are just imagining the possibilities and what you want. Improving Efficiency, Scalability, and Getting everybody on the same page.

What is the Purpose of the Tool?

To discover every single element that you can do better, faster, easier, cheaper, and do it right which is better than what anyone else is doing out there. This tool was designed with the intent to get everyone on the same page because to get everyone on the same page, you must create the page first. That's what I created.

What to fill out?

This tool is best filled out in a team setting when everyone involved in the process is present in the room. It can be filled out in Excel or PDF or handwritten or done on the whiteboard on the wall. You can utilize the tool as a resource on where to direct your thinking.

Where to direct your thinking while utilizing the thinking tool?

When filling out each step, ask yourself what the ideal outcome is and why is this step necessary. Is it essential? Can we do without it? If not, how can we do it most effectively? Is that the highest level of effectiveness? Who is the ideal person to do it? What is the ideal time frame? Go deep on each step of the process. Most of the world is going shallow and the ones that go deep see a breakthrough and become pioneers and disruptors.

Some Questions that you can ask yourself at each step when using The Process Innovator™:

What would be an ideal or dream come true result for this step?

What would you imagine to be the most effective way to achieve the ideal result in the most effective, least time-consuming, and easiest way?

What would need to be true to achieve that ideal result?

Is this step even necessary? Can we eliminate this step?

How are we doing it right now? What is causing it to be done it that way right now? What needs to change or be improved to be done in the most ideal way?

Are we doing it in the ideal time frame? What would be the ideal time frame? Who would be the right person to do it in the ideal time frame? What activities does that person need to free up from to accommodate this if they are currently not doing this?

Where are we stuck in this step? Why are we getting stuck? Who can make us unstuck if we don't know how?

What would be the time and money investment you or the company would be willing to make to build the new changes or improvements?

The Process Innovator™

Step No. 10	What's the next step and its ideal outcome?

Finish: Ideal Result?

What are the top 5 elements that have to be true?	What are the top 5 obstacles you faced or will face in the journey?

How will you achieve this outcome most efficiently?

Who? (Position/s) — Time: H/D/W/M

Step No. 9	What's the next step and its ideal outcome?

How will you achieve this outcome most efficiently?

Who? (Position/s) — Time: H/D/W/M

Top 1-5 Strategies to improve your process	Who	What	Wl

Step No. 8	What's the next step and its ideal outcome?

How will you achieve this outcome most efficiently?

Who? (Position/s) — Time: H/D/W/M

Step No. 7	What's the next step and its ideal outcome?	Step No. 6	What's the next step and its ideal outcome?

How will you achieve this outcome most efficiently?

Who? (Position/s) — Time: H/D/W/M

How will you achieve this outcome most efficiently?

Who? (Position/s) — Time: H/D/W/M

The Process Innovator™

Process Name: _____
Prepared By: _____
Start Date: ___/___/___ End Date: ___/___/___

Start	What's the step and its ideal outcome?

How will you achieve this outcome most efficiently?
Who? (Position/s)   Time: H/D/W/M

Step No. 1	What's the next step and its ideal outcome?

How will you achieve this outcome most efficiently?
Who? (Position/s)   Time: H/D/W/M

Top 3 Insights	Actions

Step No. 2	What's the next step and its ideal outcome?

How will you achieve this outcome most efficiently?
Who? (Position/s)   Time: H/D/W/M

Top 6 to Strategies to Improve your process	Who	What	When

Step No. 3	What's the next step and its ideal outcome?

How will you achieve this outcome most efficiently?
Who? (Position/s)   Time: H/D/W/M

Step No. 5	What's the next step and its ideal outcome?

How will you achieve this outcome most efficiently?
Who? (Position/s)   Time: H/D/W/M

Step No. 4	What's the next step and its ideal outcome?

How will you achieve this outcome most efficiently?
Who? (Position/s)   Time: H/D/W/M

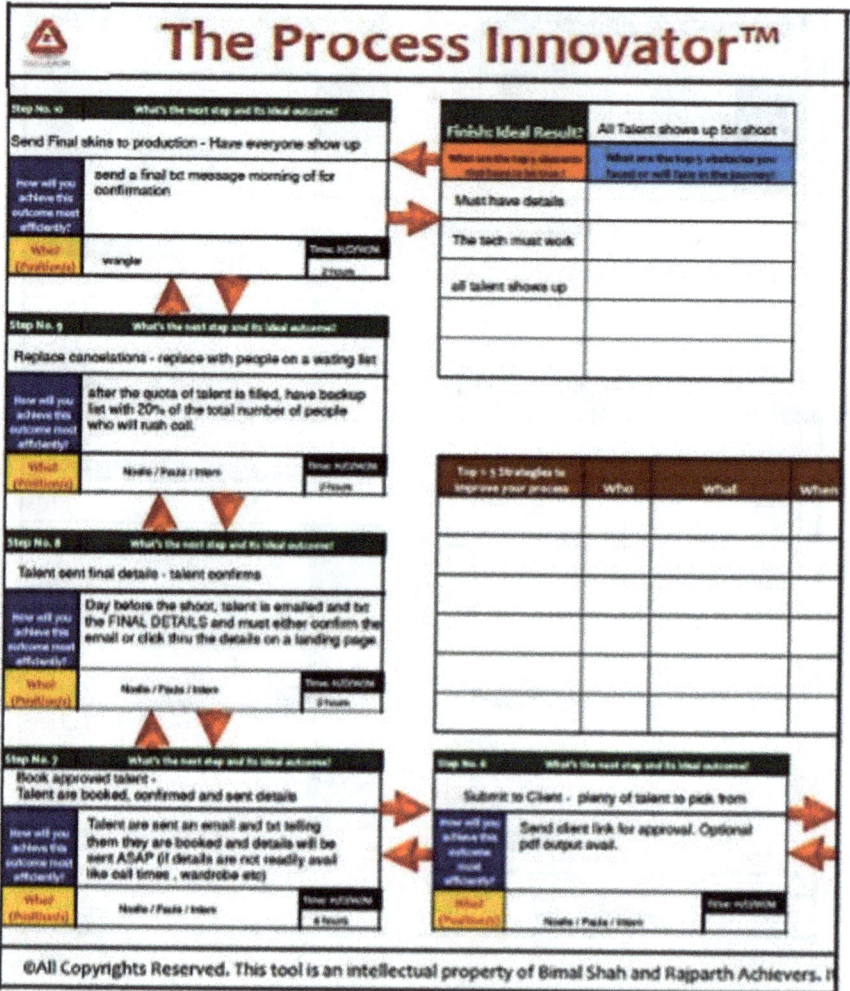

The Process Innovator™

Step No. 10	What's the next step and its ideal outcome?
Send Final skins to production - Have everyone show up	

How will you achieve this outcome most efficiently?	send a final txt message morning of for confirmation

What (Position/s)	wrangler	Time: H/D/W/M 2 hours

Step No. 9	What's the next step and its ideal outcome?
Replace cancelations - replace with people on a waiting list	

How will you achieve this outcome most efficiently?	after the quota of talent is filled, have backup list with 20% of the total number of people who will rush call.

What (Position/s)	Noelle / Paula / Intern	Time: H/D/W/M 2 Hours

Step No. 8	What's the next step and its ideal outcome?
Talent sent final details - talent confirms	

How will you achieve this outcome most efficiently?	Day before the shoot, talent is emailed and txt the FINAL DETAILS and must either confirm the email or click thru the details on a landing page

What (Position/s)	Noelle / Paula / Intern	Time: H/D/W/M 2 Hours

Step No. 7	What's the next step and its ideal outcome?
Book approved talent - Talent are booked, confirmed and sent details	

How will you achieve this outcome most efficiently?	Talent are sent an email and txt telling them they are booked and details will be sent ASAP (if details are not readily avail like call times, wardrobe etc)

What (Position/s)	Noelle / Paula / Intern	Time: H/D/W/M 6 Hours

Finish: Ideal Result?	All Talent shows up for shoot

What are the top 5 elements that have to be true?	What are the top 5 obstacles you faced or will face in the journey?
Must have details	
The tech must work	
all talent shows up	

Top 1-5 Strategies to improve your process	Who	What	When

Step No. 6	What's the next step and its ideal outcome?
Submit to Client - plenty of talent to pick from	

How will you achieve this outcome most efficiently?	Send client link for approval. Optional pdf output avail.

What (Position/s)	Noelle / Paula / Intern	Time: H/D/W/M

©All Copyrights Reserved. This tool is an intellectual property of Bimal Shah and Rajparth Achievers. I

16

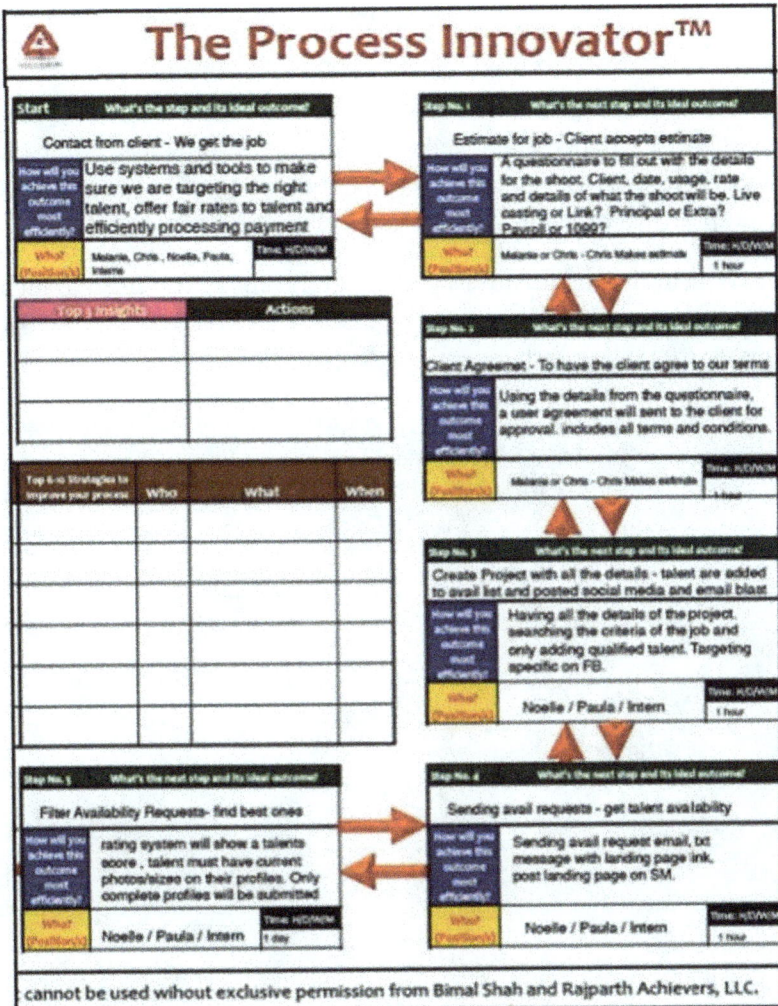

Now that you have understood how to utilize processes in building your leap, you must make a list of all the processes you would need to build. To do the same, you ought to know the

misunderstanding you might have of the leap as an entrepreneur. That misunderstanding is that you might try to jump standing up. Try to jump standing up and see how far or how high you will go. You will not go that far or that high.

You need to take twenty or more steps backward and run up to the point from where they want to jump and then jump far. If you want to jump high, you need a lever to jump high. When you run, you need to be fit to make that jump. In the same way, your business must be fit to make that sprint.

So, to effectively leap in any aspect of your business, you need to identify the areas that your business is unfit and the steps you need to take back to run up to the point where you can leap.

What are the top ten to twenty steps your business needs to take backward to take an effective leap forward?

1. _____

2. _____

3. _____

4. _____

5. _____

6. _____

7. _____

8. _____

9. _____

10. _____

11. _____

12. _____

13. _____

14. _____

15. _____

16. _____

17. _____

18. _____

19. _____

20. _____

Steps here could be, you need to improve your customer service, so you can retain your customers. Or you need to invest in building your online presence to give your business much-needed visibility.

It could be that you need to deliver a better-quality product or service experience, or your business model of pricing needs to change. All those are steps that you are taking backward to move forward. So, taking a step back just means you are thinking deeply about each aspect of your business.

Taking 20-30 steps backward here means, you should do an audit of your business, and identify the areas that you need to give more momentum to, for example, your hiring process, operations, marketing, and sales, and you do the needful to boost them, so when you combine all the improved momentum in all aspects of your business, it can enable you to take a major leap forward in your business.

In Book #3, I have provided all the 12 essential functions and a scorecard to help you discover what the gaps are in your business. This can help you focus on all the specific steps you need to take up to the point from where you can make that leap.

Nevertheless, you can follow the steps below and try to build specific steps in a few areas and replicate the process. Think of three to five gaps you would like to fill in your business, and then identify the necessary things you need to put in place, to enable you to fill those gaps to scale forward.

Business Gap #1:

The strategy that will allow you to fill that gap most effectively:

Steps you need to take to implement that strategy:

Business Gap #2:

The strategy that will allow you to fill that gap most effectively:

Steps you need to take to implement that strategy:

_____
_____
_____
_____
_____

Business Gap #3:

_____
_____
_____
_____
_____

The strategy that will allow you to fill that gap most effectively:

_____
_____
_____
_____
_____

Steps you need to take to implement that strategy:

_____
_____
_____
_____
_____

Business Gap #4:

_____
_____
_____
_____

The strategy that will allow you to fill that gap most effectively:

_____

_____

_____

_____

_____

Steps you need to take to implement that strategy:

_____

_____

_____

_____

_____

_____

Business Gap #5:

_____

_____

_____

_____

_____

The strategy that will allow you to fill that gap most effectively:

_____

_____

_____

_____

_____

Steps you need to take to implement that strategy:

_____

_____

_____

_____

_____

_____

For example, if you have been unable to get a loan for your business because of your credit score, fixing your credit score and deleting the inaccurate items from your credit report is the step you are taking backward to move a step forward and open a world of opportunities with healthy credit. Healthy credit is one area of business being fit.

Your overall business needs to be fit and healthy too in all other areas and you must define what a healthy business is to you as it is different for different entrepreneurs.

In your own words, define your healthy business:

According to an article written by Lauren Schreiber[1] titled "What makes a healthy business? An internal control perspective", a business can be said to be healthy if it is constantly adapting and adjusting to the environment in which it operates. The article further went on to say that a company's ability to react to change is impacted by its resources, and these resources do not only refer to cash at hand but also current information on the company's performance. Because without proper systems in place, it may be tricky to understand the resilience of your business when the time comes to react to changes in the business environment.

I will let you in on one secret of this leap. Every change that you make in your business for the leap, becomes part of your business DNA so it can sustain for a long time. This is the beauty of backward steps that are making you go forward on a continued basis.

To build the healthy business that you defined earlier, you need to identify the areas of your business that are unhealthy.

Write down five to ten areas that you believe are unfit and unhealthy in your business:

1. _____

2. _____

3. _____

4. _____

5. _____

6. _____

7. _____

8. _____

9. _____

10. _____

It could be your marketing messages that are confusing and don't provide clarity to the audience as to what you are all about. It could be that you have the wrong people working for you. Whatever it is, you need to confront it and make the essential changes.

So now, after identifying the top one to five areas in your business, that are unfit, you need to brainstorm on the three steps you can take in each to leap towards becoming healthy in those areas. This can be a collaborative effort that involves a team working together in those areas.

If you're having trouble with this, please see the example given after the exercise.

First Unhealthy area in your business:

_____

_____

The strategy that will allow you to make that area healthy most effectively:

_____

_____

_____

_____

_____

Three steps to implement that strategy:

1._____

_____

2._____

_____

3._____

_____

Second Unhealthy area in your business:

_____

_____

The strategy that will allow you to make that area healthy most effectively:

_____

_____

_____

_____

_____

Three steps to implement that strategy:

1._____

_____

2._____

_____

3._____

_____

Third Unhealthy area in your business:

_____

_____

The strategy that will allow you to make that area healthy most effectively:

_____

_____

_____

_____

_____

Three steps to implement that strategy:

1._____

_____

2._____

_____

3._____

_____

Fourth Unhealthy area in your business:

_____

_____

The strategy that will allow you to make that area healthy most effectively:

_____

_____

_____

_____

_____

Three steps to implement that strategy:

1._____
_____

2._____
_____

3._____
_____

Fifth Unhealthy area in your business:

_____
_____

The strategy that will allow you to make that area healthy most effectively:

_____
_____
_____
_____
_____

Three steps to implement that strategy:

1._____
_____

2._____
_____

3._____
_____

So, let's say for example that one of the identified unhealthy areas in your business is Marketing, you need to ask yourself, what are my competitors doing in their marketing, that is making them dominate the market share?

The other big reason your marketing may not be working is because of the messaging and sequencing to your highest lifetime value.

Another thing that a business needs to be able to leap high is a stick. Not just any stick, but a leverage stick, and you can build this stick. Book #3 is all about building your lever and fulcrum and leveraging your strengths. It goes significantly in depth. In this book, you can look at four areas, namely, people, strategy, execution, and cash to understand and build your leverage stick to jump high.

To build strong leverage, you need to first face your understanding of leverage. What is your understanding of leverage?

_____
_____
_____
_____
_____

Leverage according to the Cambridge dictionary is using something that you already have, to achieve something better. It could also mean that something you can build so you have a strong lever.

So, what leverage does your business currently have?

_____
_____
_____
_____
_____

Think of things you have in your business, that you can use to your benefit. All these are things that you can leverage upon, to take a major business leap.

In your own words define a leverage stick.

_____
_____
_____

You can build your leverage stick from four areas - people, strategy, execution, and cash. These four areas if used effectively, will enable you to have a leverage stick, that can help your business make a major leap and achieve the 90-Day Leap.

To build the most effective and optimal leverage stick in those four areas, you will have to refer to books #1 through 5 to understand the people you need to count on or people you need to hire, the strategies you need to build, how to build the most optimal execution, and with the right amount of cash.

I will need you to go back and read your answers to the questions in those books, as they will help you identify the top 10 people you need to be working with, within or outside your company to build your leverage stick. As well as come up with 10 strategies, 10 ways of execution, and 10 ways to increase your cash flow. You can do this as a brainstorming session with your team.

Who are the top one to ten people you need to work with to build your leverage stick?

1. _____

2. _____

3. _____

4. _____

5. _____

6. _____

7. _____

8. _____

9. _____

10. _____

What are one to ten strategies you can use to increase your leverage?

1. _____

2. _____

3. _____

4._____

5._____

6._____

7._____

8._____

9._____

10._____

What are one to ten ways you can execute your strategies to increase your leverage?

1._____

2._____

3._____

4._____

5._____

6._____

7._____

8._____

9._____

10._____

What are one to ten ways you can increase your cash flow in your business?

1._____

2._____

3._____

4. _____

5. _____

6. _____

7. _____

8. _____

9. _____

10. _____

Kudos on completing week one, where you learned how to make "the fit business" leap. Cash flow is everything in business and when you have great cash flow you feel like you are in heaven. I want you to get the cash flow you need to be supercharged and have the fuel to take off. In the next chapter, I will teach you about the three-bucket cash flow heaven.

Before you head off to week two, please check out the next page, where you will have the chance to write the takeaways from this chapter that can assist you in leveraging your topmost strengths and working on strengthening the lever and the fulcrum in the next 90 days; this will greatly facilitate in achieving your three-year goal in one year.

P.S.: attached on the next page are useful resources that you should check out, as they will be of immense help to you.

Week 1

Your Chapter Dominoes

What are your top 5 STEPS that will deliver the highest payoffs, fill the widest gaps, and make you leap the farthest?

1. _____
   _____
2. _____
   _____
3. _____
   _____
4. _____
   _____
5. _____
   _____

Please fill in the quadrant with the Top 5 in each category to build your lever to jump the highest:

People		Strategy	
1		1	
2		2	
3		3	
4		4	
5		5	
Execution		Cash Flow	
1		1	
2		2	
3		3	
4		4	
5		5	

Useful Resources

QR Code to scan and get all FREE Tools and Resources:

Link from the QR Code:

https://linktr.ee/TheOneYearBreakthrough

Link to all my events:

https://www.eventbrite.com/o/bimal-shah-7943115300

Time to Celebrate

Before you move to the next chapter, take time to celebrate.

Here are five little ways you can celebrate:

1. Go Big- Get Pure 22 Karat Gold Jewelry for your better half.
2. Go watch a show at Improv Theatre.
3. Dance in the rain created from your hose on your favorite song.
4. Paint something or have a painting time with Family.
5. Eat Fresh and Hot Krispy Kreme Doughnuts.

Week 2

The Three-Bucket Cash Flow Heaven

Like you, I used to think that you need to spend money to make money. Soon I realized that the business would consume as much money as you invest in it. If you are not properly converting it into sustainable cash flow, you will be out of money in no time. Then I learned that cash flow is everything and that the key to making a successful leap is your cash flow. The runway that you want to take off from when you want to fly (leap), is your cash reserves. The key to building cash reserves is your cash flow. If there is solace and hardship in business, it is cash flow. Have you ever felt the same? I feel that way, so I developed a system to make you feel like you are in your best comfort zone with your business. The system is the Three-bucket cash flow system.

I built this three-bucket system to simplify it for myself and help entrepreneurs like you. We have been using that and over three years it has benefitted to such a point that our credit score has gone up by 275 points to the highest it can be.

I can share another story as well. About 2 years ago, using the three-bucket system, I increased the cash reserves of the company by more than 10-fold from just a mere $20,000 to $270,000 in 90 days purely from proper cash management. Their business also as a result was on track to be more than doubling as they were set to grow at more than 50 percent a quarter using the "fit business" leap. Their business grew from $1.8 Million to $5 Million in a year and had the best year ever in 20 years in the business.

Below I would walk you through a series of mindset exercises, tools, and the next steps in building The three-bucket cash flow heaven.

Do you have a systematic percentage or a system to set aside money for business reserves? ☐ Y ☐ N

If not, do you currently have business reserves (not personal reserves) that are at least 3 months of your monthly operational expenses? ☐ Y ☐ N

If yes, then that is great. You can use the system to improve your cash reserves and take it to the next level. If not, you can build the reserves that you need. The key to building company cash reserves is also financial habits. One key habit is the habit to set aside money no matter what every month.

Do you have a habit to set aside money every month? ☐ Y ☐ N

If yes, please continue to the next steps. If not, please build those habits using the essential financial behavior tool at: https://bit.ly/EssentialMoneyHabits
You may ask, if I am not putting all my resources into the business, what should I do then? Ideally, you should maintain a minimum of six months of operating expenses in business reserves or the specific amount of reserves you need for your long-term 5-year Moonshot. You also don't want to use retirement plans or other accounts meant for your kids' education as reserves.

Let's understand your current reserves. To know the number of resources you have, and what to allocate to your business, you need to do an inventory of all your liquid resources. Let's do that now.

How much cash do you have on hand?

This is cash from all your bank accounts, cash equivalent accounts like money market accounts, and is readily accessible to you. Please do the math and write it down.

Others would count as a line of credit, the cash value of personal life insurance policies as cash reserves, and SBA Loans that you may maintain in an account. Many banks even count that when making lending decisions. I personally only believe that cash on hand is the only true cash reserve of business. All others shouldn't be counted as cash reserves for the reasons outlined below.

Line of credit can be canceled or converted into an outstanding loan or mortgage. The cash value of life insurance is a personal asset and should remain as a personal asset and SBA Loans can be called or become due because of a circumstance in your business so you shouldn't count those. SBA loan stands for Small Business Administration loan that can be issued by banks or the government directly and backed by the strength and credibility of the SBA. This allows banks to share the risk on the loans with the SBA and that's why they prefer issuing SBA loans to business owners.

Kudos on completing the above tasks, now let's look at the second fundamental principle of a business- Your customer value.

The second fundamental principle of a business is the customers' ITV (Initial Transaction Value), ATV (Annual Transaction Value), and LCV (Lifetime Customer Value)

ITV simply stands for your customer's initial transaction value, that is the amount the customer is bringing into your business for the first transaction they would do with you to begin the relationship. You can plan a complete journey from the beginning to the beginning. Yes, you read that right "beginning to the beginning"- this is a way you can retain a customer for life and a very long time. Every journey's end that you plan should lead to the beginning of a new journey that the customer can hop on to. Thus, you plan a recurring revenue for the customer that can keep on going. Sell the Journey and not the product or service. You can use the "Building The During Unit Tool" below to plan that journey:
https://bit.ly/DreamCustomerExperience

For example, if the journey that you build for your customer experience begins with an initial transaction of $1,000, the $1000 being paid here is the initial transaction value of the customer.

Please calculate below.

What would be your ideal ITV and what is your current ITV and how would you get to your ideal ITV?

_____
_____
_____
_____

ATV simply stands for your customers' annual transaction value. This is the total dollar value of all the transactions that your customers can do in the journey that you built using the tool above. The more optimal you build the journey, the higher your ITV and the higher your ATV would be. You can look at the way your current ATV stands by looking at the average ATV of all the customers. It may be skewed if you have some very high-paying customers and some very low-paying customers. In that case, you can use the arithmetic mean. Please calculate below.

What would be your ideal ATV and what is your current ATV and how would you get to your ideal ATV?

_____
_____
_____
_____

LCV simply stands for your customers' Lifetime Customer Value. This is the total dollar value of all the transactions that your customers can do over their entire lifetime of them being a customer with you before they exit or stop doing any business. The more optimal you build the journey, the higher your LCV would be. You can look at the way your current LCV stands by looking at the average LCV of all the customers. It may be skewed if you have some very high-paying customers and some very low-paying customers. In that case, you can use the arithmetic mean. Please calculate below.

What would be your ideal LCV and what is your current LCV and how would you get to your ideal LCV?

_____

_____

_____

_____

The customers' lifetime value can transform your business to the next level and chasing that can completely transform your business to the next level in the fastest and most optimal way. The key element is do you believe the same. Let's answer that.

Why do you believe you need to find a way to chase your customer's optimal ITV, ATV, and LCV?

_____

_____

_____

_____

_____

Once you have grounded that belief in your head, you are ready to incorporate that into your 90-Day leap and find out what projects would lead to that.
What are the top 5 projects that would lead your company to achieve your customer's optimal ITV, ATV, and LCV?

1._____
2._____
3._____
4._____
5._____

Once you have derived these values, you would know how many customers you need to pay off any debt obligation. For example, if your debt is $100,000, if your 1st transaction is $1,000, and your ATV is $5,000, then you need 22-23 customers -if there are expenses you will need higher- Please refer to your ideal P&L statement, you built in book four of this series titled capturing your biggest opportunities.

After calculating the number of customers, you will need to be able to settle your debt obligations and other expenses, you then need to build a list of your ideal 5-star prospects for your business. You can build that at: https://bit.ly/5StarProspects

After doing this, we can then move on to the third fundamental principle of a business.

The third fundamental principle for your business is to not run out of cash by letting your revenues drive your expenses and not the other way around. To make sure you have your revenues driving your expenses, make sure you have at least three customers that are your ideal customers and have those three refer you to the other three, and so on. Once you derive revenue from those, you can look at your P&L and see how much funds to spend in your business on marketing, advertising, technology, new hires, and so forth.

Understanding customer value is very essential to the three-bucket cash flow system. This way you will know how many customers you need to bring into the journey to get to the cash flow you want and what to do with that cash flow. To make the 90-day leap in four weeks, your business cash flow needs to be positive. If your cash flow is negative, you need to go back to Book # 4 and discover how to bring your negative cash flow into a positive.

Many businesses fail because they do not have a strong handle on their cash flow, and often money gets misused for different objectives and that's when problems start happening. This is why the three-bucket system is so valuable. It will help you take major leaps you can just keep on growing in leaps and bounds.

However, once you become a big corporation, you will have to structure something very different, and I can help you with that. But this strategy I want to share with you will at least get you started to the point that you can grow to the next level.

You will have to first divide your business cash flow into three buckets, namely: Operations, Growth, and Reserve.

The first bucket named operations, signifies your day-to-day operational expenses that you need to maintain to continue your business. This doesn't include expenses that you spend for growth namely marketing, technology, new hires, and initiatives that are planned for growing the business. This includes what it would take to run your business at the level it is and give you your paycheck as well that you take for your living expenses.

Based on the description above, what are your monthly operational expenses? $_____

The next step is to open a business bank account for operations and have that monthly amount that you need on the 1st of the month. If you cannot have those funds at the beginning of the month, you should understand the timing of all your payments and those dollar amounts at the beginning of each week.

Funds that you must have at the 1st of the month.
$_____
Or
Funds that you must have at the beginning of the 1st week.
$_____
Funds that you must have at the beginning of the 2nd week.
$_____
Funds that you must have at the beginning of the 3rd week.
$_____
Funds that you must have at the beginning of the 4th week.
$_____

The second bucket named growth signifies your vision for the company and your clearly defined goals for the company. You need to refer to book #1 or get book # 1 and build your 25-Year Vision, 5-Year Moonshot, 3-Year Goal, and The One-Year Breakthrough. Based on the breakthrough plan, you need to set aside your growth goals for each month and the money that would be needed in that bucket.

Based on the description above, what is your monthly growth investment? $_____

The next step is to open a business bank account for growth investment and have that monthly amount that you need on the 1st of the month. If you cannot have those funds at the beginning of the month, you should understand the timing of all your payments and those dollar amounts at the beginning of each week.

Funds that you must have at the 1st of the month.
  $_____
or
Funds that you must have at the beginning of the 1st week.
$_____
Funds that you must have at the beginning of the 2nd week.
$_____
Funds that you must have at the beginning of the 3rd week.
$_____
Funds that you must have at the beginning of the 4th week.
$_____

The third bucket named reserve is where you keep 6 months' worth of operational expenses, in case you run out of cash, or you need money to be funded into the business. Ideally, you can also fund six months of your growth expenses into your reserve, so in case of severe economic or business downturns, you have the fuel to adapt, pivot, change, learn, and improve to sustain and scale your business.

The analogy here is that running a business can be related to flying a plane. And you can't fly a plane with an empty or half-full tank, you need a full tank and enough in the reserve to fly a plane. The cash reserve is also for your runway. You can't fly a plane without a runway and the cash reserve serves the dual purpose of the runway and the fuel in the tank. Also, you need to make sure you have enough money in your business reserve account so you can effectively run your business despite any issues you may face.

Based on the description above, what is your ideal reserve account balance and what is your current reserve account balance?
$_____

The next step is to have a separate business bank account for reserves. You may feel why to open all these bank accounts. The reason is I have experienced the proper results and so have my small and big business clients by having three separate bank accounts. You can have all the accounts in the same bank to transfer money easily or set up auto-transfers. It also becomes so much easier to make the right financial decisions. If you are at the ideal reserve account balance or higher, great. You can use the tool on the next page to improve your growth investment and reserve account balance. If not, you can use the tool to get to the balance by the date you set below:

By what date will you have the ideal reserve account balance?
___/___/_____

The Business Cash Flow Management System™

Name: _____
Start Date: _____ End Date: _____
Project: _____

What will be your monthly operations account spending you have to adhere to every month? (A)	How Much do you get in monthly bank deposits or gross profit? (B)	Amount that you will maintain in your Reserve account (from A x 3 to A x6)	Monthly Deposit on the 1st of every month to make in your Operations Account (A)	Monthly Growth budget available (B-A) to deposit on the 1st on every month	How would you allocate the monthly planning budget to meet your goals?
					Machinery, Licensing, Advertising on Print and
$35,000	$55,000	$105,000	$35,000	$20,000	Online, E-commerce

Operations Account Monthly Deposit	Growth Account Monthly Deposit and planned withdrawals		Reserve account Maintenance strategy	
	$4,500 Advertising, $1,000 on Machinery lease payments, $5,000 for licensing for 6 months		Auto transfer $25,000 as soon as balance drops to 50,000	
$10,000	$2,000 for e-commerce, balance set aside to build reserve account to $105,000		$20,000 auto-transfer for 3 months.	

TM & © Rajparth 2014-2020 Rajparth Achievers, LLC. This integral concept may not be reproduced in any way shape or form without the written permission of the Publisher, Rajparth Achievers, LLC. Made in Florida, USA.

TRANSFORM

The Business Cash Flow Management System™

Name: _____
Start Date: _____ End Date: _____
Project: _____

What will be your monthly operating expenses that you have to adhere to every month? (A)	How Much do you get as monthly deposits in bank or Gross Profits? (B)	Amount that you will maintain in your Reserve account (from A x 3 to A x6)	Monthly Deposit on the 1st of every month to make in your Operating Account (A)	Monthly Growth budget available (B-A) to deposit on the 1st on every month	How would you allocate the monthly growth budget to meet your goals?

Operations Account Monthly Deposit	Growth Account Monthly Deposit and planned withdrawals	Reserve account Maintenance strategy

All the systems I present won't work if you don't believe in them. It becomes essential for you to review your own beliefs by writing them down.

What are your beliefs about having a proper cash-flow system to manage your business finances and why do you have the above belief?

Are the above beliefs you wrote down useful in helping you achieve the goals that you want? ☐ Y ☐ N

If yes, great use them. If not, you must change your belief system and adapt to the beliefs that will help you get what you want.

Your reserves help you get out of problems, help you sustain your business in slow times, and help you recover when your business is not doing well, or when you don't have a business for a month.

Do you believe a business can combine its operations and growth account? ☐ Y ☐ N

If yes, that's not a good idea, and I will explain why that is so below.

If not, why do you believe so?

Combining the operations and growth accounts is not a good idea, as you may run short on money to cater for operational costs because you have spent all of it on the growth aspect of your business. Separating the two helps you maintain a steady cash flow in the business and most importantly make the right financial decisions in a very easy manner.

For the growth account, you must divide the money into separate components to cater to the different goals needed to help you achieve your business vision for a year. And you will have a clear budget of what you're going to do, every month for that year.

What goals do you have for your business that will help you make major leaps and what growth dollars do you want to allocate to each?
1._____ Growth $_____
2._____ Growth $_____
3._____ Growth $_____
4._____ Growth $_____
5._____ Growth $_____

Following this strategy of dividing your business cash flow into three buckets, will help you grow your business in major leaps. So now, let's look at strategies that will help you put this system on autopilot for your business.

Now that you know the amounts you need in each bank account on specified dates, you can do the autopilot in two ways.

Strategy # 1 The easiest way is to set an auto-transfer at the beginning of each month from the accounts to the other accounts and put it repeatedly with no end date. This way you have set it and forget it.

Strategy # 2 If your cash flow is not sufficient to do the transfers on autopilot on the 1st of the month, then you need to do a deep dive into the timing of your cash flows each month. If each month is different and you have no idea, you must do a deep dive into the type of customers and how much they pay you when and what percentage you can transfer to other accounts when you receive them.

I can share a quick story on strategy #2. There was a restaurant owner who was running a negative cash flow each month and drying up his personal savings. He was getting scared he would run out of money. What we did was allocate percentages of each type of revenue stream and transfer them to separate accounts. For example, a big portion of the catering revenue would go into reserve accounts that he wouldn't touch as the catering business is like a windfall.

Then we took a percentage of daily credit card transactions, cash transactions, and buffet days and put percentages for each. We soon realized that the buffet was good for cash flow as there were fewer service people needed and there were more customers at that time. We increased the buffet days by just one additional day a week and his business quickly turned positive with good operations, growth, and reserve account balances.

How can you put your business cash flow management system on auto-pilot?

_____
_____
_____
_____
_____
_____
_____
_____
_____
_____

You can also follow some of the steps below to set up your autopilot system:

1. Type of revenue: _____
   % to allocate to Growth Account: _____
   % to allocate to Reserve Account: _____

2. Type of revenue: _____
   % to allocate to Growth Account: _____
   % to allocate to Reserve Account: _____

3. Type of revenue: _____
   % to allocate to Growth Account: _____
   % to allocate to Reserve Account: _____

You can also try another strategy that is fixed dollar amount based on assured recurring revenue that you have coming in:
1. Assured Recurring Revenue: _____   Date: _____
   $ to allocate to Growth Account: _____
   $ to allocate to Reserve Account: _____

2. Assured Recurring Revenue: _____   Date: _____
   $ to allocate to Growth Account: _____
   $ to allocate to Reserve Account: _____

3. Assured Recurring Revenue: _____   Date: _____
   $ to allocate to Growth Account: _____
   $ to allocate to Reserve Account: _____

Your operations account is where all the cash flow for the business comes in and from there you would set up all the transfers to the other two accounts. What you do is every month, when cash comes into your account, you allocate the ones for operations and growth and the remaining one goes into the reserve, some banks offer the service of when your reserve account drops below a fixed amount, there's an auto-transfer schedule, or you can schedule a transfer every month from your growth bucket, until the reserve account reaches the specified amount, and then you allocate your growth resources, and start working towards achieving your growth plan.

Now I want to help you develop a personal cash flow management system. Understanding that cash flow is the most important thing when you're looking at your life and making sure that it's on autopilot.

Having a personal cash flow management system helps you maintain your cash flow and achieve your objectives on a day-to-day basis, to make sure you're not exceeding your budget and going into debt, or doing things that you don't want or will later regret because you did it.

Just like we created three different bank accounts for your business, you would open three different bank accounts for your personal expenses. You would have a lifestyle, goals, and emergency account.

The lifestyle would be for your personal lifestyle for the life that you want to live. If you want to take vacations every month, you should budget it in your budget and make it part of your budget. If you would like to dine at some of your favorite restaurants or new restaurants every weekend, budget it as part of your lifestyle. If you like to and want to go shopping, do your manicure, or pedicure often, budget it, and make it part of your lifestyle.

Based on the above, what is needed for your monthly lifestyle?
$_____

The goals account is based on your personal goals. For example, you may want to buy a home in six months and need to accumulate funds for a down payment.
You may consider buying a car soon and may need funds for that.
You may need to set aside every month for your retirement, your kid's college education, paying down your debt or credit cards, and other goals that you might have. All those payments should happen from this account. So, you know what you need for your growth account every month.

Based on the above, what is needed for your monthly goals account?
$_____

Your emergency account should be ideally six months of your lifestyle account needs. You can title your emergency account as Wages account because of garnishment protection against wages offered by the Consumer Credit Protection Act, Title III. According to CCPA, Title III[2], * a major portion of your wages can be protected if they are above $217.50 weekly and cannot be garnished by creditors. So, if you have up to six months of your wages directly deposited into your Wage account, you can protect that and use that for emergencies.

Based on the description above, what is your ideal emergency account balance and what is your current emergency account balance?
$_____

If you are not at the target balance, what is a date by which you believe you would be able to reach that? _____

Please use the tool on the next pages to plan your cash flow.

The Cash Flow Management System™

Name: _____
Start Date: _____ End Date: _____
Project: _____

What will be your monthly lifestyle spending that you will adhere to every month? (A)	How Much do you get paid every month (B)	Amount that you will maintain in your Emergency account (from A x 3 to A x6)	Monthly Deposit on the 1st of every month to make in your Lifestyle Account (A)	Monthly planning budget available (B-A) to deposit on the 1st on every month	How would you allocate the monthly planning budget to meet your goals?
					Education, retirement, Investments, Life Insurance, Tax Planning, Estate Planning, Gifting
$10,000	$25,000	$50,000	$10,000	$15,000	

Lifestyle Account Monthly Deposit	Planning Account Monthly Deposit and planned withdrawals		Emergency account Maintenance strategy
	$2500 Tax-free retirement, disability, estate planning, and insurance, $2000 education, $8,500 retirement		Auto transfer $10,000 as soon as balance drops to 40,000
$10,000	$2000 gifting		$15,000 auto-transfer for 3 months.

The "Auto-Pilot" Cash Flow Management System™

Name: _____
Start Date: _____ End Date: _____
Project: _____

What will be your monthly lifestyle spending that you will adhere to every month? (A)	How Much do you get paid every month (B)	Amount that you will maintain in your Emergency account (from A x 3 to A x6)	Monthly Deposit on the 1st of every month to make in your Lifestyle Account (A)	Monthly planning budget available (B-A) to deposit on the 1st on every month	How would you allocate the monthly planning budget to meet your goals?
					Education, retirement, Investments, Life Insurance, Tax Planning, Estate Planning, Gifting.
$10,000	$25,000	$50,000	$10,000	$15,000	

Lifestyle Account Monthly Deposit	Planning Account Monthly Deposit and planned withdrawals		Emergency account Maintenance strategy
	$2500 Tax-free retirement, disability, estate planning, and insurance, $2000 education, $8,500 retirement		Auto transfer $10,000 as soon as balance drops to 40,000
$10,000	$2000 gifting		$15,000 auto-transfer for 3 months.

TRANSFORM

Thumbs up on completing week two, where you learned how to make sure you have a system to manage and improve your cash flow, and the steps to indicate you're over-crushing your target.

In the next chapter I will teach you about the scale-ready recurring leap algorithm, I am sure you're excited to know what it's about. You will earn about a systematic way to make recurring leaps where each leap is better than the previous one. You will discover how to write one-line business plans with algorithms.

Before you head off to week three, please check out the next page, where you will have the chance to write the takeaways from this chapter that can assist you in managing and improving your cash flow, putting it on autopilot, and working on the most favorable cash flow revenue opportunities in the next 90 days; this will greatly facilitate in achieving your three-year goal in one year.

P.S.: attached on the next page are useful resources that you should check out, as they will be of immense help to you.

Week 2

Your Chapter Dominoes

What is your ideal ITV, ATV, and LCV?

$_____; $_____; and

$_____

What would be the top 5 strategies to get to your ideal ITV, ATV, and LCV in the next 90 Days?

1. _____

_____

2. _____

_____

3. _____

_____

4. _____

_____

5. _____

_____

Please fill in the quadrant with the info in each category for putting your managing your cash flow and putting it on autopilot:

Your Business Cash Flow Buckets	Your Personal Cash Flow Buckets
Operations Account: $_____	Lifestyle Account: $_____
Growth Account: $_____	Goals Account: $_____
Reserve Account: $_____	Wage (ER) Account: $_____
Your Top 5 Strategies for Cash Flow on Auto-Pilot	Your Top 5 Strategies for Cash Flow on Auto-Pilot
1	1
2	2
3	3
4	4
5	5

Useful Resources

QR Code to scan and get all FREE Tools and Resources:

Link from the QR Code:

https://linktr.ee/TheOneYearBreakthrough

Link to all my events:

https://www.eventbrite.com/o/bimal-shah-7943115300

Time to Celebrate

Before you move to the next chapter, take time to celebrate.

Here are five little ways you can celebrate:

1. Buy tickets to a favorite show that is an hour or more away from where you live and take your better half to that place on a date night.
2. Go divulge yourself to eating the best chocolates at a specialty chocolate shop.
3. Buy your better half his or her favorite perfume.
4. Set up 12 recurring date nights on your calendar and plan for at least 6 of them.
5. Order Dry Erase Paint on the wall that is closest to your home office.

Week 3

The One-Line "Scale-ready" Algorithms

I used to wonder how companies scale and grow big. I used to always have this doubt that there is no way that they would have the time to write extensive elaborate 200 to 500 pages business plans for each initiative. There must be another way. One day when I was going through my old college projects, I discovered one of the theses I had written and built a brand-equity index. It was a one-line representation of a brand's position in the industry. I thought why this same method can't be applied to business? "Eureka!" I screamed. Then I discovered the one-line business plans.

The one-line plan is an algorithm that is written in a mathematical style. Your business has a lot to do with mathematics. Have you ever thought of an algorithm for your business? Not just any algorithm but a "scale-ready algorithm"? A "scale-ready" leap algorithm is something that you can fill in the blanks and you can use as often as you need. An algorithm is a process or a set of rules you follow in a sequence with certain calculations and weightage to succeed.

Once it works one time, you improve and apply it for the next one. Scale-ready means that it allows you to rapidly grow using a system. It puts you on the highway instead of driving in your neighborhood where you can only drive at 15-25 miles an hour.

Let me share a quick story on the scale-ready recurring leap algorithm. When we did the fit business leap for an FBA e-commerce business (Fulfillment by Amazon), we discovered the scale-ready algorithm was in the culture, reviews, pictures, descriptions, and product launches. We designated one person as the astronaut whose sole job was product launches on Fridays. We trained everybody on the team to be a photographer with a 'Picture Scorecard'. Every Wednesday was a picture day. The product launches tripled, we built a great culture, got walkie-talkies to improve communication, and more than doubled the sales in the first 90 days of training. We all celebrated in Margarita Ville Resort for the weekend with extended family. The company has grown 3X with that algorithm and now has grown 10X and still uses the algorithm every time. Below was their one-line algorithm:

$$\text{W} + \text{D} + \text{F} + \text{M} = \$1.3\text{M}/\text{Q}$$

Below I would walk you through a series of questions, exercises, thinking tools, and the next steps to help you build your own One-line "Scale-ready Leap Algorithm".

The key foundation to building your algorithms is to think in 90-Day time frames. There can't be any excuses for this. This is essential. Think about all the companies that release their quarterly earnings report and there is expected to be stock movement during the release of the quarterly earnings. No matter how good or bad the quarter went at the end of the quarter, the true report is due for that quarter, and you start planning for the next quarter. If it is great, you can say "Let's plan the celebration and do even better the next quarter and have a bigger celebration for the next one."

If it is bad or not so good, "It is what it is. Let's adapt, pivot, learn, change, improve, or do whatever we need to for the next one to make it better."

The concept of thinking in 90 days comes from the fact that 90 days is the range where planning and ambition fall reasonably close together. It gives the perfect time frame for you to have an idea of what you want to get done, as you can estimate your capacity reasonably well and make huge strides and leaps toward your major long-term goal. This helps you move faster without compromising strategy.

With that in mind, do you agree to plan and execute each of your leaps in 90-Day time frames no matter what? ☐ Y ☐ N

If Yes, that's great. If not, you can go through the questions below to shift your thinking:

Give three to five reasons Why 90-day goals are beneficial to your business?

1. _____

2. _____

3. _____

4. _____

5. _____

Life changes a lot in a year, especially in the life of a start-up, so sometimes setting annual goals only is not ideal, as those goals might not be relevant by the 11th or 12th month. Also, sometimes the small-scale business owner may view 12 months as a long time and figure out that they can always start tomorrow which never comes. Also, it lets you know if your plan is going to fail, as you will be able to fail quickly and re-strategize appropriately. Also, the 90-day time frame allows you to plan strategically for each week for 12 weeks with The Daily Accountability Report that you can get from your team with the tool that you will come across in this chapter soon.

With The Daily Accountability Report, you are targeting each one of your team members to achieve six victories every day. If you multiply the six victories by the number of people you have in your team and 90 days, you can imagine how many victories you would have by the end of the quarter.

The tool systematically focuses on two aspects- bringing money into the business and taking the business to the next level. Imagine you and each one of your team members focusing on those two aspects of the business throughout the day. You can see results that are way beyond your expectations. When you want your team to be productive, you give them less and get more in that less than you give to them. Have your team go deep in each of the targeted six victories to achieve the highest result possible every day.

I have my quote: "What gets measured and reported daily, takes improvement to a whole new level." –© Bimal Shah.

To utilize The Daily Accountability Reporting Tool, you need to set three short-term victories and three long-term victories for yourself, and you need to do little things daily to ensure you achieve them.

What are 3 short-term victories you would like to achieve every day in the week that will put money in the bank for the business?

1. _____

_____

_____

2. _____

_____

_____

3. _____

_____

_____

What are 3 long-term victories you would like to achieve every day in the week that will take the business to the next level?

1. _____

_____

_____

2. _____

_____

_____

3. _____

_____

_____

With the victories you have outlined above, you are now ready to use The Daily Accountability Reporting tool on the next pages which can also be replicated for each of your team members.

The Daily Accountability System™

Prepared for Bimal Shah

Start Date: 02/28/2020   Target Weekly Score: __20__ (COVID-19 Week 2)   End Date:03/28/2020

Day	Targeted Short-Term Results (Money In The Bank)				Targeted Long Term Results (Next Level Growth)				Your Daily Score	Insights With Next Best Action- Who needs to do what by When
	No.	Y/N	0/1	Legitimate Explanation IF NO	No.	Y/N	0/1	Legitimate Explanation IF NO		
M o n	1	Yes	1		1	Yes	1		2	
	2	Yes	1		2	Yes	1		2	
	3	Yes	1		3	Yes	1		2	
T u e	1	Yes	1		1	Yes	1		2	
	2	Yes	1		2	Yes	1		2	
	3	Yes	1		3	Yes	1		2	
W e d	1	Yes	1		1	Yes	1		2	
	2	Yes	1		2	Yes	1		2	
	3	Yes	1		3	Yes	1		2	
T h u	1	Yes	1		1	Yes	1		2	
	2	Yes	1		2	Yes	1		2	
	3	Yes	1		3	Yes	1		2	
F r i	1	Yes	1		1	Yes	1		2	
	2	Yes	1		2	Yes	1		2	
	3	Yes	1		3	Yes	1		2	
S a t	1	No	0	Other elements in this list took priority	1	Yes	1		1	
	2	Yes	1		2	No	0	Other elements in this list took priority	1	
	3	No	0		3	Yes	1		1	
Total		16				17			33	

©All Copyrights Reserved. This tool is an intellectual property of Bimal Shah and Rajparth Achievers. It cannot be used without exclusive permission from Bimal Shah and Rajparth Achievers, LLC.

So now that you know the importance of thinking in 90-day time frames, Is there anything holding you back from doing it?

_____

_____

_____

_____

_____

_____

Do you think 90 days is too short to leap? ☐ Y ☐ N

If yes, then you are incorrect. 90 days are sufficient to leap- all you must do is decide where you can and where you cannot make a leap and plan accordingly. If not, you are on the right track.

When creating 90-day plans for your business, it's important to consider various factors, including time, personnel, finances, and personal factors.

I ask that you be open to the idea, because breaking your one-year major goal into 90-day goals, will help you achieve your one-year goal faster, as you may find out that by diligently carrying out your 90-day goal, you may be able to achieve your 1-year goal in 6 months. Also, you can find out that a goal you intended to achieve in one year, might take two years, so you will be able to know this early and re-strategize accordingly. If not, that's great, get started on making 90-day plans for your business.

The next step is goals. What are the top two to five goals you intend to achieve in the next 90 days with your business?

1. _____

2. _____

3. _____

4. _____

5. _____

On the goals that you wrote above, one of the absolute key elements is having the right people in the right seats.

Do you have the right people in the right seats or the right team to help prepare and accomplish your 90-day plans? ☐ Y ☐ N

If yes, kudos, you have ticked this off the to-do list of factors needed to prepare and accomplish your 90-day plans. If not, you need to look for the right people, they could be internal or external people.

One of the fatal mistakes you can make is not knowing who you want. This is why I created a tool for the same.

Below is a link to the **FREE** tool to discover who you really want in your team: https://bit.ly/MyDreamEmployee. You can keep using the tool for as many positions as you need to fill until you get the system.

From the tool you have used above, I need you to think of the top two to five positions and people if you happen to know for those positions you will need to have onboard to help you prepare and work with you to achieve your 90-day goals.

No	Position	People you might know
1		
2		
3		
4		
5		

So, some of you may say you don't know the people you need to work with right now to achieve your goals, and that's okay. Let me help you out here, I want you to think of your goals in parts, and the different sub-teams that will be needed to achieve those goals, list out the top two to five sub-teams:

1. _____

2. _____

3. _____

4. _____

5. _____

After listing out the top two to five top sub-teams you need to achieve your goal, I need you to research the best people that you have access to in those fields that need to make up your sub-teams, these are the people that should be part of your team.

The next factor we will look at is money.

Do you have the financial resources to plan and achieve your 90-day plan? ☐ Y ☐ N

If yes kudos, you are on your way to achieving your goals. If not, you need to find a way to get the money, I have already shown you this in week 2 of this series. As well as tell you how to create a growth budget for your plans.

Next, it's important to consider your personal hurdles.

Are there any personal obstacles preventing you from creating and accomplishing your goals? ☐ Y ☐ N

If not, kudos, you should get started on getting your plans in motion.

If yes, what personal obstacles are holding you back?

There are physical hurdles and there are psychological hurdles. If you have physical hurdles, I can certainly understand, and you must give the time and care that is needed to overcome those hurdles. If you have psychological hurdles, you can overcome those with this mindset shift tool that I have developed:

https://bit.ly/TheHiddenShift

With this tool, many clients have seen that hidden shift in their mindset that has completely changed their perspective.

So now, let's dive into the second aspect of this week 3, which is learning ways to incorporate some concepts into your life that will help you to make 90-day leaps a recurring habit.

One of the elements of the algorithm is to set BHAG®[3] (Big Hairy Audacious Goals)[3] Goals. The BHAG® Goals can be revenue, profitability, operational excellence, marketing, or anything that you believe that you want your business to achieve that will take it to the next level.

The BHAG® Goals were originally developed by Jim Collins and Jerry Porras. BHAG ® Goals are useful in that it's a long-term goal that everyone in a company can relate to, and rally behind it. Simply put, a well-thought-out BHAG ® shifts everyone in the company's focus to the bigger picture. And it is meant to energize and excite people in a way that lengthy mission statements and quarterly targets often fail to do.

Are the goals you defined earlier BHAG® Goals? ☐ Y ☐ N

If yes, that's great. If not, please rewrite your goals to make sure they are BHAG® Goals:

1._____

2._____

3._____

4._____

5._____

If a business can successfully execute a BHAG®, it can prove to be the cornerstone for a tremendous achievement. Now, I want to walk you through setting Red, Yellow, Green, and Super-green milestones for each quarter.

A red zone is a danger zone that can comprise 50 percent achievement of the goals you set or 50 percent of some of the goals that you set. One goal you should absolutely include is the one that relates to cash flow i.e., revenue or gross profit. Red zone means the company completely missed its targets by a significant amount and it seriously needs to evaluate its people, strategy, execution, and finances.

It is essential to build your own custom red zone (danger zone) definition. In 90 days, what would make you consider your company to be in the red zone?

_____

Now that you have defined the red zone, to build it into your one-line algorithm, you would fill in the blanks below:

____R–

The blank before the R is the percentage of your goals you would consider to be in the red. The superscript is the number of factors that must be at that percentage for you to consider your company to be in the red.

Example: $50R^3$

Ideally, when a company is in the red, you wanted to look at everything and everyone with a microscope to discover what went wrong. You would deeply evaluate every aspect of your business. How did you get there?

The next step is to define what steps you would take if your company was in the red zone:

If a company is in Red, it needs to do a microscopic evaluation of all four elements- People, Strategy, Execution, or Cash.

Based on what you defined above, you can come up with a one-line algorithm for what causes the company to be in the red:

___P + ___S - __E - __C = $50R^3$

In the above example, the bank before P stands for the number of people who didn't do what they were supposed to do. The blank before S stands for failed strategies, E stands for the non-executed strategies, and C stands for percentage overspent on expenses that didn't give the expected ROI (Return on Investment) or any ROI (Return on Investment).

The next step is to do your own custom one-line algorithm for Red below:

_ _

Now let's look at the yellow zone. A yellow zone is a caution zone that can comprise either 80 percent achievement of the goals you set or 80 percent of some of the goals that you set. It should however be at a minimum a breakeven zone for cash flow. Yellow zone means the company just reached 80 percent of its intended milestones and a breakeven point in the finances.

It is essential to build your own custom yellow zone (caution zone) definition. In 90 days, what would make you consider your company to be in the yellow zone?

_ _

_ _

_ _

_ _

_ _

_ _

_ _

Now that you have defined the yellow zone, to build it into your one-line algorithm, you would fill in the blanks below:

____Y--

The blank before the Y is the percentage of your goals you would consider to be in Yellow. The superscript is the number of factors that must be at that percentage for you to consider your company to be in the red.

Example: $80R^5$

Ideally, when a company is in the yellow, you wanted to look at where you need to adapt, where you need to pivot, what you need to change, what did you learn, and what you need to improve. You must look at how did you get there?

The next step is to define what steps you would take if your company was in the yellow zone:

_____
_____
_____
_____
_____
_____

If a company is in yellow, it needs to do an evaluation on all four elements- People, Strategy, Execution, or Cash plus what it can adapt, pivot, learn, change, or improve.

Based on what you defined above, you can come up with a one-line algorithm for what causes the company to be in the yellow

$$\_\_\_P + \_\_\_S - \_\_E - \_\_C = 80R^5$$

In the above example, the bank before P stands for the number of people who didn't do what they were supposed to do. The blank before S stands for failed strategies, E stands for the non-executed strategies, and C stands for percentage overspent on expenses that didn't give the expected ROI (Return on Investment) or any ROI (Return on Investment)

The next step is to do your own custom one-line algorithm for Yellow below:

_____

Now let's look at the Green zone. A Green zone is a Celebration Zone that can comprise 100 percent achievement of the goals you set. It should however be at a minimum at 95 percent of the targeted revenues or gross profits. Green zone means the company just reached 100 percent of its intended milestones and improved profitability points in the finances. In this Zone, the company should plan out a celebration for the whole team. It could be as simple as a dinner with the team or a bowling night or could be as lavish as your company can go with the amount of money you can spend. An investment in the team to make them happy can make the company grow beyond its imagination. A happy team means a happy company and it means happy clients.

It is essential to build your own custom Green Zone (Celebration Zone) definition. In 90 days, what would make you consider your company to be in the Green zone?

_____

_____

_____

_____

_____

_____

_____

Now that you have defined the Green zone, to build it into your one-line algorithm, you would fill in the blanks below:

_____G--

The blank before the G is the percentage of your goals you would consider to be in Green.
The superscript is the number of factors that must be at that percentage for you to consider your company to be in the red.

Example: $100G^5$

Ideally, when a company is in the Green, you wanted to look at What worked, and what didn't work, KWINK (Knowing What I Now Know) What would I do differently or would have never started, and who needs to do what by when?

The next step is to define what steps you would take if your company was in the green zone:

_____

_____

_____

_____

_____

_____

If a company is in green, it needs to celebrate, and you need to write how would you be willing to celebrate with your whole team.

_____
_____
_____
_____
_____
_____

Based on what you defined above, you can come up with a one-line algorithm for what causes the company to be in the Green

$$\_\_\_P + \_\_\_S + \_\_E + \_\_C = 100G^5$$

In the above example, the bank before P stands for the number of people who did do what they were supposed to do. The blank before S stands for successful strategies, E stands for the fully executed strategies, and C stands for expenses that did give the expected ROI (Return on Investment)

The next step is to do your custom one-line algorithm for Green below:

_____

Now let's look at the Super-Green zone. Yes, Super-Green is a color for purposes of business. It is a color of your own choice. It could be gold, could be dark green, or whatever you choose. A Super-Green zone is a Super Celebration Zone that can comprise 125 percent achievement of the goals you set or higher. It should however be at a minimum at 115 percent of the targeted revenues or gross profits. Super Green zone means the company exceeded its intended milestones and improved profitability points in the finances. In this Zone, the company should plan out a BIG celebration for the whole team. It could be as simple as a three-day weekend stay at a resort or a one-day all-day outing like a fishing trip on a yacht or could be as lavish as your company can go with the amount of money you can spend. An investment in the team to make them happy can make the company grow beyond its imagination. A happy team means a happy company and it means happy clients.

It is essential to build your own custom Super Green Zone (Celebration Zone) definition. In 90 days, what would make you consider your company to be in the Super Green zone?

Now that you have defined the Super Green zone, to build it into your one-line algorithm, you would fill in the blanks below:

_____SG--

The blank before the SG is the percentage of your goals you would consider to be in Super Green. The superscript is the number of factors that must be at that percentage for you to consider your company to be in the red.

Example: $125SG^5$

Ideally, when a company is in the Green, you wanted to look at What worked, and what didn't work, KWINK (Knowing What I Now Know) What would I do differently or would have never started, and who needs to do what by when?

The next step is to define what steps you would take if your company was in the super green zone:

If a company is in super green, it needs to celebrate BIG, and you need to write how would you be willing to celebrate BIG with your whole team.

Based on what you defined above, you can come up with a one-line algorithm for what causes the company to be in the Super Green

___P + ___S +__E +__C = 125G^5

In the above example, the bank before P stands for the number of people who did do what they were supposed to do. The blank before S stands for successful strategies, E stands for the fully executed strategies, and C stands for expenses that did give the expected ROI (Return on Investment)

The next step is to do your custom one-line algorithm for Super Green below:

Now below put the SUPER GREEN FORMULA IN BOLD AND BIG LETTERS. Please share it with your Team as well

Kudos on completing week three, where you learned how to rapidly grow your business, year in, and year out using a system. In the next chapter, I will teach you about the one-page 90-Day Blueprint, to help you make your 90-Day leap. Do check out the free resources provided for your good on the next page, before rushing off to week four.

In the next chapter, I will teach you about the ultimate one-page 90-Day leap that puts everything that you have learned from Books 1 through this chapter on a single page. Mind-blowing isn't it!!- Combine 6 books worth of knowledge and takeaways on ONE PAGE!!, I am sure you're excited to know what it's about. You will learn how this one-page tool is better than many detailed business plans that just give information but no substance that can turn into results.

Before you head off to week four, please check out the next page, where you will have the chance to write the takeaways from this chapter that can assist you in the ONE LINE Algorithms for your business and you can easily crank them out for any aspect of your business; this will greatly facilitate in achieving your three-year goal in one year.

P.S.: attached on the next page are useful resources that you should check out, as they will be of immense help to you.

Week 3

Your Chapter Dominoes

What is YOUR 150% SUPER GREEN ALGORITHM?

_____

How would you celebrate if you achieved 150% SUPER GREEN?

_____

_____

_____

_____

_____

Who would be the potential Top 3 to 5 Team members who can get you 150 Percent of Super Green and a Bonus for each?

1. _____ *Bonus: $_____*
2. _____ *Bonus: $_____*
3. _____ *Bonus: $_____*
4. _____ *Bonus: $_____*
5. _____ *Bonus: $_____*

Useful Resources

QR Code to scan and get all FREE Tools and Resources:

Link from the QR Code:

https://linktr.ee/TheOneYearBreakthrough

Link to all my events:

https://www.eventbrite.com/o/bimal-shah-7943115300

Time to Celebrate

Before you move to the next chapter, take time to celebrate.

Here are five little ways you can celebrate:

1. BONUS YOURSELF!
2. Have a pillow fight with your spouse for fun.
3. Have a Dress Competition at home with your family for fun.
4. Dine at Six Tables Restaurant
5. Have 2 shots of your favorite Tequila.

Week 4

The One-Page 90-Day Blueprint

I used to initially think every plan in business needs a detailed business plan. It also used to bug me that if you had to spend weeks and maybe months preparing everything, when will you be able to implement it? I started imagining there must be something better. At that time, there was my one-page house blueprint on my desk, and I wondered If your house can be built with a blueprint, why can't you build your business with a One-Page blueprint? I looked at how the house blueprint had different sections and different drawings for each and how they were connected, and I started building the same for business. I always thought about business in 90-day intervals, So, I developed a 90-day blueprint for the business. This week you are going to walk away with that one-page 90-day blueprint that puts it all together.

With this one-page blueprint, there are so many companies that have benefited and so can you. I know one solopreneur who used this one-page blueprint to grow from being solo to a team of four, take his first vacation in 7 years, and grow from 60,000 to 600,000 in less than a year. You can make that big leap too!

Below I would walk you through a series of questions, exercises, thinking tools, and the next steps to help you build that one-page 90-Day blueprint.

To build the 90-Day blueprint, we would put all the work together of consolidating all of what you have learned in the earlier books of this series of Vision, Dangers, Opportunities, Strengths and managing their weaknesses and using the gained knowledge in building the 90-Day Leap.

It is essential that you take your dominoes from each of the earlier books and each of the chapters and use those to build your blueprint.

Let's walk through all the dominoes that you built in the earlier books:

Domino # 1 from Book #1:

Your 3-year Vision that is integrated into your 5-year Moonshot and 25-Year Character Vision:

_____

_____

_____

_____

_____

_____

_____

_____

_____

_____

Domino # 2 from Book #1:

Your "One-Year Breakthrough Plan" to achieve your three-year goal in one year.

_____

_____

_____

_____

_____

_____

_____

_____

_____

Domino # 3 from Book # 2:

Your Three Biggest Pains:

1._____
_____
_____
_____
_____

2._____
_____
_____
_____
_____

3._____
_____
_____
_____
_____

Domino # 4 from Book # 2:

Your Three Biggest Frustrations:

1._____
_____
_____
_____

2._____
_____
_____
_____

3._____
_____
_____
_____

Domino # 5 from Book # 2:

Your Three Biggest Challenges:

1._____
_____
_____
_____
_____

2._____
_____
_____
_____

3._____
_____
_____
_____
_____

Domino # 7 from Book # 2:

Your strategies or systems that will relieve each of your three biggest pains:

1._____
_____
_____
_____
_____

2._____
_____
_____
_____

3._____

_____

_____

_____

_____

Domino # 8 from Book #2:

Your strategies or systems that will eliminate each of your three biggest frustrations:

1._____

_____

_____

_____

_____

2._____

_____

_____

_____

_____

3._____

_____

_____

_____

Domino # 9 from Book #2:

Your strategies or systems that will resolve each of your three biggest challenges:

1._____

_____

_____

_____

_____

2._____
_____
_____
_____
_____

3._____
_____
_____
_____
_____

Domino # 10 from Book #3:

Your three biggest Dangers (Your weaknesses that can become threats to you):

1._____
_____
_____
_____
_____

2._____
_____
_____
_____
_____

3._____
_____
_____
_____
_____

Domino # 11 from Book #3:

Your three biggest Obstacles that you need to overcome:

1._____
_____

_____

_____

_____

2._____

_____

_____

_____

_____

3._____

_____

_____

_____

_____

Domino # 12 from Book #3:

Your three strategies or systems to eliminate each of your dangers most effectively:

1._____

_____

_____

_____

_____

2._____

_____

_____

_____

_____

3._____

_____

_____

_____

Domino # 13 from Book #3:

Your three strategies or systems to overcome each of your obstacles most effectively:

1._____
_____
_____
_____
_____

2._____
_____
_____
_____
_____

3._____
_____
_____
_____
_____

Domino # 14 from Book #4:

Your three biggest opportunities that you need to capture:

1._____
_____
_____
_____
_____

2._____
_____
_____
_____
_____

3._____
_____
_____
_____
_____

Domino # 15 from Book #4:

Your three strategies or systems to capture your biggest opportunities:

1._____
_____
_____
_____
_____

2._____
_____
_____
_____

3._____
_____
_____
_____
_____

Domino # 16 from Book #5:

Your Strongest and Optimal Lever:

_____
_____
_____
_____
_____

Domino # 17 from Book #5:

Your Ideal Fulcrum:

_____
_____
_____
_____
_____

Domino # 18 from Book #5:

Your three biggest strengths that you can leverage using Your Lever and Your Fulcrum:

1._____
_____
_____
_____
_____

2._____
_____
_____
_____
_____

3._____
_____
_____
_____
_____

Domino # 19 from Book #5:

Your WMD System:

_____
_____
_____
_____
_____
_____
_____
_____
_____
_____

Domino # 20 from Book #5:

Your strategies or systems to leverage each of your three biggest strengths:

1._____
_____
_____
_____
_____

2._____
_____
_____
_____
_____

3._____
_____
_____
_____
_____

Now, you need to take each of the strategies that you wrote for each of the dominoes and allocate the people, projects, time, and money for each. Each system, structure, capability, resource, strategy, or the "how" or "who" is a project. Projects are what will take your business to the next level. You need to do fewer tasks and more projects. It will make you accomplish one milestone after the other. In the table below you need to collate all the strategies you wrote to incorporate in the one-page 90-day leap blueprint:

Domino # 21: Your Top 20 Strategies/Systems from all 5 books:

No	Strategy/System	Project Name	Team	Time	Money IN	Money OUT
1						
2						
3						
4						
5						
6						
7						
8						
9						
10						
11						
12						
13						
14						
15						
16						
17						
18						
19						
20						

After you have done this, you are ready to build The One-Page Blueprint on the next pages.

The Biggest 90-Day Leap™

Achieve Your Three-Year Goal in One Year

Name:_____

Start Date: _____ End Date: _____

If we were to meet here THREE Years from today, and you were to look back over those THREE YEARS to today-- What has to have happened during that period, looking back to today, to make you feel that you had a meaningful transformation personally and professionally speaking?	

What are your Biggest Frustrations, Pains, or Challenges?

Your Biggest Frustrations, Pains, or Challenges	Result or Solution you need	Who	What	When?

Your Biggest 90-Day Leap

What are your biggest Projects you need to work on?	Ideal Result You would like to achieve?	By when would you like to achieve	Team that will assist you in achieving that result

Total

The Biggest 90-Day Leap™

Achieve Your Three-Year Goal in One Year

Name:_____
Start Date:_____
End Date:_____

What insights did you gain from the book/workshop?	

What will assist you in making the leap towards your three-year goal?

What are the biggest Dangers you face that	What are the biggest	What are the biggest strengths that you

Your Investment

Time you would need to Allocate	Time your team would need to Allocate	Your Financial Gain or Value from the end result	The Net Investment You are willing to make to achieve that end result

At this juncture, I want to congratulate you for achieving a successful leap. You should reward yourself for getting started on this journey of successfully building the system of recurring 90-day leaps.

You have learned and discovered a timeless system that you can keep using quarter after quarter for decade after decade until you are in business. It's time to reward yourself for this big victory and milestone.

You want to celebrate BIG. So, write your celebration below. How would you like to reward yourself for this GREAT milestone?

Kudos on completing this chapter, where you learned how to build The One Page 90-Day blueprint. I wish you all the best on this wonderful journey you're embarking on. Cheers to major leaps in your business every quarter. Remember, if you fall short of your goals, there's always another quarter.

In the next book, I will teach you about converting your 90-day leaps into 12 Proactive Weekly Sprints to make sure you have a system to proactively track and achieve your milestones. Imagine you have a foolproof system to execute everything!! I am sure you're excited to know what the book will be about.

But, before you head off to Book # 7, please check out the next page, where you will have the chance to write the takeaways from this chapter that can assist you in never forgetting what your "One Page 90-day Leap Blueprint" is all about. It will also be the driving motivator for you to chase and achieve that 90-day leap.

P.S.: Do check out the free resources provided for your continued success on the next page.

Week 4

Your Chapter Dominoes

Your meaningful driver for the 90-Day Leap:

Your Projects Time IN	Your Money IN	Your Money OUT

Your transformative driver for your TEAM for the 90-Day Leap:

Your Team Projects Time IN	Your Money IN	Your Money OUT

Useful Resources

QR Code to scan and get all FREE Tools and Resources:

Link from the QR Code:

https://linktr.ee/TheOneYearBreakthrough

Link to all my events:

https://www.eventbrite.com/o/bimal-shah-794311530

Time to Celebrate BIG!!

Before you move to the next chapter, take time to celebrate BIG as you
have learned a foundational system for sustainable scalability.

Here are five little ways you can celebrate:

1. TAKE YOUR DREAM FAMILY VACATION!
2. Plan your dream Staycation.
3. Plan a gathering for all your family and relatives that you may not have
met for decades.
4. Go to an exquisite furniture shop to get some nice furniture for your
home.
5. Travel on a long flight in First Class-it is fun!

Doubling Your Business and Taking Over Your Industry in a Year!
Hidden Insights from this Book

Below, I have provided proven uncharted bottom-line insights from this book to double your business and rise in your industry in a year:

1. The "FIT Business Leap":

Just like you need to stay hydrated to stay fit and your business needs to stay hydrated. Hydrate also comprises the most essential elements for your business- H-Hire the right people, Y- Your business is your personality, D-Daily Outcomes, R-Reporting systems, A- Accountability for Self and Team, T-Teamwork including you, E-Exponential Growth is the key- don't target linear growth.

2. The Three-Bucket Cash-Flow System:

You can divide every line item in your P&L Statement into three buckets:
1.   Who or what team is responsible for it?
2.   What is the ideal amount?
3.   What system, structure, or strategy will get you the ideal amount?

3. The One-Line "Scale Ready Algorithms":

You can create "One Line Scale Ready Algorithms" for many aspects of your business. You just need to know the elements that make it whole. You just need to take it as a puzzle and gather all the pieces. The easiest formula you can apply is P_2TM_2. This is a puzzle that you can easily figure out.

4. The One-Page 90-Day Leap Blueprint:

Now that you are trained, you can build a one-page 90-Day leap Blueprint in 90 minutes to 3 hours depending on the complexities. All you must do is remember the Vision, Pains, Challenges, Frustrations, Dangers, Opportunities, Strengths, People, Projects, Time, and Money.

DON'T FORGET

Join The Pioneers Club for FREE!

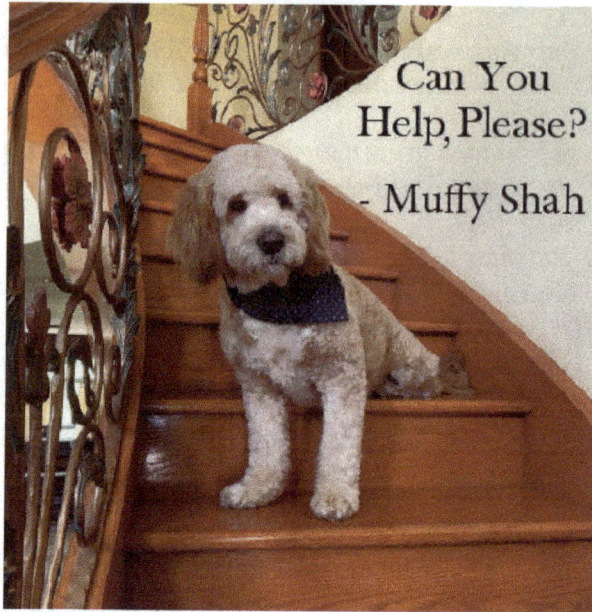

Can You
Help, Please?

- Muffy Shah

Thank You for Reading My Book!

I appreciate your reading this book!

I would love it if you can give me an honest review.

I need your input to make the next version and my future books better.

Please leave me a helpful 5-Star review on Amazon, letting me know.
what do you think?

Thank you so much!
—Bimal Shah

Please don't forget to check out the next book—on making the optimal weekly sprints for your 90-Day Leaps.

This is the next step in the sequence of steps to Becoming a Pioneer by achieving your three-year goal in one year.

See you in book 7!

DON'T FORGET

Join The Pioneers Club for FREE!

With the purchase of each book, you are Eligible to Join the Club Meeting for FREE

Connect with Pioneers around the World—Every Month. With the book purchase, you are a member. No strings attached.

Connect with Me and walk away with personalized insights for you in the Club meetings held every month on Wednesdays at 6 PM EST.

Walk away with a customized 30-Day Action Plan at each meeting.

Get Your FREE Membership at: https://bit.ly/ThePioneersClub.

Conclusion

My dear friend and business owner we have come to the end of book 6. It's been a wonderful journey. This book if used appropriately will help you make your ideal 90-Day leaps in not only your business but in your personal life.

The book asks deep questions that call for self-reflection. Please take your time to go through the questions, perform the exercise given, and fill in the tools provided. Because they will help you greatly in achieving major leaps in your business and life.

I believe that I have given you everything I can to help you make the optimal leaps in your business, and this will help you achieve your full entrepreneurial potential and be the Pioneer God called you to be.

Bye for now. See you in book seven.

About the Author

Bimal Shah is an accomplished Senior Executive, Entrepreneur, Advisor, Coach, and Results Leader with more than twenty years of success in the financial services industry. Leveraging extensive experience in growth, entrepreneurship, talent development, financial reporting systems, profitability systems, and processes to

scale, he is an asset for companies spanning various industries, sizes, and stages of growth that are seeking expert assistance in bringing their business to the next level. His broad areas of expertise include executive coaching, strategic planning, operations management, scaling, and growth.

As a breakthrough coach, Bimal has successfully helped companies generate growth of more than 50 percent in a year and has taken 26 companies to exponential growth in a year. Through his unique hiring process technique, he has helped dozens of companies hire highly qualified C-Level employees. He has worked with more than fifty companies, providing coaching and financial consulting services across an array of industries, including manufacturing, distribution, home health care, communications, security systems, and professional services. His unique Coaching-Planning-Accountability system has generated favorable results in record time for CEOs, reducing their working hours, in six months, by 35 percent.

As a result, CEOs see exponential company growth within a year, can hire smart and productive team members at all levels within a few months, and receive the tools to develop effective "out of the box" marketing strategies.

Bimal is also the founder of Rajparth Advisory Group (2005), which provides financial consulting services to entrepreneurs. From 1996 to 2005, before founding Rajparth Group, he worked as an independent advisor through Northwestern and New York Life, helping more than 1000 families preserve their assets, reduce their taxes, increase their income, and create everlasting legacies.

During his tenure, he was awarded the highest honor in the industry, The Million Dollar Round Table—Top of the Table Award for six years in a row, and Global Corporate Award for Best Life Insurance Agent in the Asian Indian Community.

Bimal has also authored and published The Daily Happiness Multiplier, available on Amazon and in bookstores throughout North America. His unique "Success Deck" consists of 52 Workshop Videos and Tools to positively impact anyone's personal and professional life with a single tool each week for 52 weeks. Bimal earned his Bachelor of Commerce in Economics from the University of Mumbai and his Bachelor of Science in Advertising from the University of Florida. He holds a Chartered Financial Consultant, Chartered Life Underwriter, and Certified Advisor in Senior Living from the American College at Bryn Mar, Pennsylvania.

Some Accolades for Bimal's Work

"Bimal is the big picture guy, and he takes us deep. I might concentrate on one idea that I think is the greatest idea in this world, and Bimal will come back with making us think 10 times bigger and he's got this amazing ability to see opportunity. He lays out a great plan to get to where you want to go and makes it just so attainable. Every entrepreneur with big goals should consider hiring Bimal and if I could have Bimal in my pocket and carry him around always that would be great."

—*Mike Barnhill, Managing Partner, Specialist ID*

"Before, I was working 70–80 hours a week. Now it is down to 45–55 hours a week. The personal impact of his coaching has allowed me to spend more time with my family. The financial impact has been priceless because of the time saved. If you are struggling, consider hiring Bimal. His books and coaching have helped me plan and organize where I want the business to go. Bimal has also taught me to push my limits and think about things more in detail on why I am doing this."

—*Reginald Andre, CEO, Ark Solvers, Inc.*

"Bimal's books and workshops have further reinforced and enhanced some aspects of my leadership; in that, he has brought on a fresh perspective on my role as a leader of the company. In addition to Bimal being a very engaging and energetic personality, he also has an open-minded and unique perspective to making learning a fun-filled experience for my staff, which then adds immeasurable value to my company."

—*Terry Sgamatto, Managing Regional Director, Seeman Holtz*

"I recently took a leap of faith . . . one that required a consistent amount of convincing myself out of a scarcity mindset and making an investment. It has just been a few weeks and I am very happy with the results of my decision. Under the advisement of Bimal, I have had to make some drastic decisions in my company but have to say overall, even though some were painful, they have all been results-driven and not emotional. I truly appreciate all that Bimal has helped me create in the first few weeks and cannot wait to see what comes next."

—*Sarah Martin, CEO, Experience Epic, LLC*

"We hired Bimal to get our company better organized and have better business practices and we have been practicing that every year for so many years now. Bimal is a pretty persistent guy, and he doesn't let us get away with being lazy. He pushed us to accomplish the goals we had set to accomplish—you helped us get it done and he didn't let us be lazy at all. If you want to build a self-managing company, Bimal is the guy-- it's worth the effort and time and it's worth the energy that you are going to put into it as you are going to get every bit and more out of it and the amount of money you spent is insignificant compared to the results you have attained. "

---*Shawn Crow, CEO, Austen Enterprises, Inc.*

Notes

1. "What makes a healthy business"
   https://www.mondaq.com/canada/credit-control-and-cash-flow/357736/what-makes-a-healthy-business-an-internal-control-perspective
   The article was published by Lauren Schreiber on December 3, 2014.

2. "Federal Wage Garnishment Law"
   https://www.dol.gov/agencies/whd/fact-sheets/30-cppa
   United States Department of Labor, October 2020.
   Consumer Credit Protection Act's Title III (CCPA)

3. "Big Hairy Audacious Goal." https://www.jimcollins.com/article_topics/articles/BHAG.html
   Copyright ©Jim Collins and Jerry I. Porras, all rights reserved. The term was originally coined by Jim Collins and Jerry Porras in their book Built to Last: Successful Habits of Visionary Companies, first published in 1994.